5 Step Marketing Plan

To Get More Customers, Referrals & Make More Money

A Winning Marketing Strategy for Small Business

By Violet James, MSM

Maximum Potential, LLC

Cover Design by Violet James

Cover Photo © masterzphotofo - Fotolia.com

You can download *5 Step Marketing Plan: A Winning Marketing Strategy for Small Businesses* in Audio version and listen on your Kindle™ tablet, iPhone®, iPod®, and Android™. To download go to Amazon.com or Audible.com or iTunes.

Table of Contents

Introduction

What is marketing? According to Wikipedia, marketing is the process of communicating the value of a product or service to customers. Put another way, marketing is helping people get what they want. WIFM- What's in it for me? People buy things they want from people they know and trust. Your goal is to get people to know you and trust you. To do this, you simply need a marketing plan that you can put into action.

One of the biggest mistakes you can make as a small business owner is to not have a marketing plan. You can have the best product or service but if customers can't find you then your competitors are gaining market share and making all the money. You have to recognize that you are in the business of not just producing products and services but in the business of **"marketing"** those products and services. Having a marketing plan is crucial to your success or failure. Once you implement a strategic marketing plan you can take your business to the next level. You will get more customers, referrals, repeat buyers and achieve more growth and success in your business.

In this book, you will have a step by step marketing plan to follow. It is recommended that you take one step at a time and do the assignment/action plan for that step before you move on. When you have completed the steps and action plans you will understand your market and competition, know your customers, have a compelling marketing message, and know how to get new customers and retain existing customers.

Let's get started!

STEP #1

Know Your Competition and What Sets You Apart

It's essential that you know and understand your market and competition. First, you have to study your local market and identify the need (problem) and the service/product (solution) that you can provide. Then it is important to study and understand who your competitors are. The more you know about your competitors the more you can differentiate yourself from them and create a niche for yourself.

Assignment #1

Conduct a **Competitive Comparison Analysis:**

List the (5) nearest direct competitors and answer the following questions for each competitor-

What you need to know about your competitors:

- Who are their clients?

- What fees are they charging and how do your fees compare?

- How are they advertising?

- What are their strengths (what are they doing well)?

1

- What are their weaknesses (what can I capitalize on)?

- Why should prospects hire you or buy from you instead of them?

Next, answer the questions on **what sets you apart from your competition-**

- How do you differ from your competitors?

- What makes you special/ unique?

- What can you offer that they don't?

NOTE:
For the complete 5 Step Marketing Plan Worksheets, go to the Appendix at the end of this book OR
to access the BONUS printable worksheets (pdf format) available, go to http://www.Relationship-ebooks.com
ENTER PASSWORD: marketing55

STEP #2

Know Your Customers

The more you know and understand about your customers (target market) the easier it is to find them and to market directly to them. Study as much as you can about your customers so you will know who your customers are, what they want, what motivates them to buy and where you can find them.

Assignment #2

Conduct a Customer Analysis:

- **Who are your customers** *(age, gender, level of education, geographical location, annual income level, ethnicity, profession, industry, job title, etc.)*?

- **Pick a niche-** Can you find a specific niche and dominate that niche? *(If you target everybody then nobody is your ideal customer. Would you rather be a small fish in an ocean or a big fish in a pond?) (Examples- Counselor that specializes in Child Therapy, Lawyer that specializes in Divorce Law, DJ for the Metro-Detroit Area).*

- **List the patterns or habits your customers and potential customers share** *(where they shop, what* *they read, watch, listen to, what social networks, websites and forums they use).*

- **List where can you find your ideal customer** *(social networks, blogs, forums, associations, events, tradeshows, etc.).*

STEP #3

Create a Compelling Marketing Message

In this step you will focus on creating a compelling marketing message and a dynamic tagline that should be included in ALL your marketing materials and promotions. You want people to not only remember your name but the benefits and results you offer them. Also, you will create an audio logo (elevator speech) that answers the question, "What do you do?" in the most effective way.

Create a **Compelling Marketing Message:**

Marketing Materials Should Focus On:

- Who your **specific** target market is
- How you can help them
- The **benefits and results** your customers receive
- A compelling reason to contact you/call to action

Marketing Materials Should NOT Focus On:

- A list of services you provide
- A complete description of your company or owner biography
- Too generic and broad target market

See examples below on the difference between listing a service/product compared to offering benefits and results:

Compare listing what you sell (the product) as "Designer Shoes" **versus** listing the benefits and results such as "Comfort for your feet & the pleasure of walking"

Compare "Used Books" versus "Hours of pleasure and benefits of knowledge."

Compare "Cottage" versus "Comfort and the quietness of a cozy place."

Compare "Business Consulting" versus "Grow your company and improve performance."

Below is an example of a very effective marketing piece that I designed for a wedding photographer. Instead of listing his services, we included a list of the benefits the customer would receive if they used his services. This advertising piece made him stand out and differentiate himself from all the other photographers at the bridal and wedding expos/shows and increased his customers significantly.

Advertising tip: It is much more effective and eye catching to add a photo in your ads.

Assignment #3

Write a list of benefits and results that you offer your customers *(brainstorming).*

Next, Create a Dynamic Tagline

A tagline defines a company/product with as few memorable, emotional, descriptive words in one short sentence.

To get inspired for your own tagline let's look at a few popular and favorite taglines:

7

McDonalds .... I'm lovin' it

Nike..............Just Do It

Allstate... ...You're in Good Hands with Allstate

M&Ms........Melts in Your Mouth,
                        Not in Your Hands

Apple.........Think Different

Assignment #4

Create a Dynamic Tagline *(brainstorming)*.

Next, Create an Audio Logo (Elevator Speech)

An audio logo is a simple statement that answers the question, "What do you do?" When answering this question most people state their job title, "I'm a designer" or "I'm a sales executive." The most effective way to answer that question is by using an audio logo. Audio logos are NOT sales pitches but instead a short 30 second statement (hook) that creates an interest for a person to want to hear more.

AUDIO LOGO: "I help *(name your target audience)* to *(name one of the benefits or results you offer)."*

Examples—
- *I consult managers in developing leadership skills and performance*
- *I teach children to stay healthy and fit*

- *I sell designer shoes for those looking for style as well as extra comfort*

Watch how an elevator pitch can change your career: http://youtu.be/8QpZ_clqwTE

Assignment #5

Create an Audio Logo *(brainstorming). If you have more than one target market you can create a different audio logo (elevator pitch) for each one.*

Now that you have created a compelling marketing message that includes benefits and results you offer and a catchy tagline make sure to include them in ALL your marketing materials. And whenever you meet someone or you are networking and they ask you "What do you do?" you will have an answer that will engage further interest and conversation.

Networking Tip: If you are networking and want to get past the "What do you do?" question then ask the question, "What do you do for fun?" This question opens up new conversations and you can find people who have the same interest as you. When you have something in common with someone they tend to like you and remember you more.

STEP #4

Determine a Marketing Budget and Marketing Mediums

In this step, you will first determine your marketing budget. How much money you have for marketing will determine what marketing mediums you will choose to use. A marketing medium is the vehicle/tool that you use to advertise and get your message out. You will want to choose a marketing medium that will give you the highest return (maximum referrals) on your investment. Your goal is to choose a medium that targets your niche prospects at the lowest possible cost. It's important to keep track of every customer/referral and know how they were referred to you.

Following is a sample list of marketing mediums:

- Internet marketing *–social media, blogs, websites, directories, twitter, etc.*
- Direct mail
- Newspaper display ads
- Strategic partners
- Public speaking
- Joint ventures
- Trade magazines
- Consumer magazines
- Association directories
- Trade show booths/ tables

- Publish articles
- Free standing inserts
- Posters
- Special events
- Movie ads
- Radio ads
- Television/Cable ads
- Publicity/Press releases
- Seminars/Workshops
- Networking
- Telemarketing/Cold calling
- Signage- Counter, Wall or Display Sign
- Window display
- Sponsorships

The most effective marketing mediums tend to be networking, strategic partners, Internet marketing, and public speaking. It's crucial in today's market for any small business to incorporate Internet marketing in their marketing plan. Internet marketing is continuously and rapidly growing and changing. There are many great resources and books on this topic available and is beyond the scope of this book.

Networking is one of the most effective marketing strategies because it can create many new business opportunities and new referrals for your business. You can find networking opportunities, for example, as a member of a local Chamber of Commerce and/or as a member of a local chapter of BNI International networking and referral groups.

Assignment #6

Develop your marketing budget *(If you have been in business for over a year, then you can easily track your marketing/advertising expense and budget. If you just started a business, then you will need to project an estimated figure).*

Assignment #7

Determine 1 to 3 marketing mediums that you will use *(A marketing medium is the vehicle/tool that you use to advertise and get your message out. Your goal is to choose a medium that targets your niche prospects at the lowest possible cost. You will want to keep track of results and drop marketing mediums that aren't doing well and add new ones until you discover the best marketing mediums that get you the desired goal for maximum referrals).*

STEP #5

Focus on (2) Essential Customer Goals

In regards to customers there are (2) main goals:

1- Get new customers
2- Retain existing customers

1. GET NEW CUSTOMERS:

After completing Assignment #7, you should have a list of 1-3 different marketing mediums you will be using. In this step, you will develop a marketing strategy with a **detailed action plan** for each marketing medium you selected.

Assignment #8

Develop (1) to (3) Action Plans to get new customers:

ACTION PLAN #1 *(brainstorming)-*

List (1) marketing strategy to get new customers *(use your assignment #7 answers as a reference)*

Note: **list only (1) strategy per action plan**

15

Examples of marketing strategies-

Increase referrals from networking *(join a membership)*

Create direct advertising campaigns *(direct mail, postcards, flyers, ads, etc.)*

Improve direct sales/networking methods *(cold calling, sales letters, trade shows, etc.)*

Increase referrals from strategic partners

Increase contacts from speaking engagements

Gain publicity *(from media coverage and/or writing books and articles)*

Find joint ventures *(marketing to customers of complementary businesses)*

Internet marketing *(create website, newsletter, SEO, open social media accounts, etc.)*

Write your GOAL *(desired outcome).*

Next, answer the following questions:

What are the **benefits** of implementing this strategy?

What are the **risks** of implementing this strategy?

What are some potential obstacles *(internal & external barriers)*? How can I overcome these obstacles?

List any resources that you can use.

List **Detailed Action Steps** and a targeted completion date for each one.

2. RETAIN EXISTING CUSTOMERS

With existing customers your goals are to have them come more frequently, have them buy more, and have them buy exclusively from you. Many businesses tend to focus on the front-end sale (initial first sale) and neglect to focus on the back-end sale (continuing stream of sales). The real money is in the back-end sales from your best, loyal customers.

Still, many businesses fail to communicate and market to their current, existing customers. I read that the average business spends six times more money to attract new customers than it does to keep old ones. Customers who already bought from you or used your services are much more likely to again as long as you offer a great product and great customer service.

To retain existing customers, first, collect your customer's contact information at the point of sale. You will want to get their name, address, phone number and email address.

It's important to get the customer's **email address** because you can market to your customer again and again at low cost. If a customer is resistant to giving their email, let them know they will be receiving special coupons, offers and discounts. That usually works.

Following are marketing strategies on how to have existing customers keep buying from you exclusively and more frequently—

- **Create a Customer Loyalty Program** – it can be a rewards program that provides discounts or perks that the customer earns by doing more business with you. It can also be a membership program that provides special incentives just for members.

- **Email Your Customers Every Month a New Promotion/Offer/Coupon** – provide your customers with special discounts every month. This strategy not only increases sales but it also keeps your name and image/brand in front of your customer constantly.

- **Include Information about Other Products/Services You Offer**- always advertise your other products/services that you offer in all invoices, mailings, emails, flyers, newsletters, advertisings, etc.

- **Have Customer Appreciation Events** – put together an event that shows you appreciate your customers and value their business. You can have a contest, offer gift prizes, bouncer for kids, food, fun, etc. People love to get together and feel a part of a community.

- **Ask for Referrals** – you would be amazed how many customers would refer your business if you just politely ask and remind them to. You can also throw in an incentive (offer a $25 gift card) for every referral you get from them as your way of saying thank you.

- **Is Anything Wrong? Cold-calling** – not everyone is comfortable with this strategy but it can be very effective for inactive customers. You would genuinely call an inactive customer and ask them "Is anything wrong?" and let them share their experience. This will give you the opportunity to explain any unintentional occurrences, if any, and convey your sincere concern for them.

Assignment #9

Develop (1) to (3) Action Plans to Retain Existing Customers

ACTION PLAN #1 *(brainstorming)-*

List (1) marketing strategy to retain existing customers per action plan-

Examples of marketing strategies-

Create a Loyalty Program
Have a Customer Appreciation Day

Write your GOAL *(desired outcome).*

Next, answer the following questions:

- What are the **benefits** of implementing this strategy?

- What are the **risks** of implementing this strategy?

- What are some potential obstacles *(internal & external barriers)*? How can I overcome these obstacles?

List any resources that you can use.

List **Detailed Action Steps** and a targeted completion date for each one.

Conclusion

One of the worst mistakes a small business owner can make is to not have a marketing plan. And still most businesses do not have one. You already have a huge advantage over your competitors because you are creating a well strategized marketing plan for your business with all the tools/steps provided in this book.

Please remember with any marketing plan you have to tweak and re-evaluate the goals/action plans. Don't give up or get discouraged when obstacles occur or you are not getting the results you want. Instead, continue to consistently implement and re-evaluate your action plans/steps and you will take your business to the next level. You will get more customers, referrals, repeat buyers and achieve more growth and greater success in your business.

May you have a winning marketing plan and much success!

Resources

US Small Business Association – www.SBA.gov offers resources on starting a business, managing a business, marketing tips, loans and grants and more.

US Chamber of Commerce- www.USChamber.com A business federation representing companies, business associations, state and local chambers in the U.S., and American Chambers of Commerce abroad.

BNI International- Business Networking and Referrals- www.BNI.com is the largest *business networking and referral marketing* organization in the world. Last year alone, BNI generated 6.9 million referrals resulting in $3.1 billion dollars' worth of business for its members. Find a local chapter in your area.

Small Business Free Marketing Courses/Programs- www.Famee.org -The Foundation for the Advancement of Marketing Excellence in Entrepreneurs is proud to offer an extensive array of resources to help small and medium sized companies improve how they grow profitable, sustainable, long-term customer revenue streams - the lifeblood of every company!

Brandeopedia – Your virtual marketing encyclopedia.

Mind Tools- www.MindTools.com -Toolkit contains more than 700 free and paid management, career and thinking skills and tools.

Free Small Business Advice- How-to Resources, Tools, Templates – www.Score.org- A nonprofit association dedicated to encouraging the formation, growth, and success of small business nationwide through counseling and mentor programs.

Market Research- Free Online Tools & Market Data – www.blog.Score.org- If you are doing market research and want to understand changing market conditions and demographic trends, market research is an essential part of your marketing/business plan.

Market Segmentation – from Wikipedia -Market segmentation is a marketing strategy that involves dividing a broad target market into subsets of consumers who have common needs (and/or common desires) as well as common applications for the relevant goods and services. Marketing campaigns can then be designed and implemented to target these specific customer segments.

Tools & Forms – BizFiling Toolkit -Free Business Template Downloads
http://www.bizfilings.com/toolkit/tools-forms.aspx

Microsoft Marketing Budget Plan- Free Template – helps you to plan your marketing budget. By filling in the planned amounts in each of the template cells, you can easily forecast what type of budget you need for marketing.
http://office.microsoft.com/en-us/templates/marketing-budget-plan-TC001145556.aspx

Microsoft Marketing Project Plan - Free Template–
small businesses can use this template to track individual
deliverables of their marketing or project plan.
http://office.microsoft.com/en-us/templates/marketing-
project-plan-TC102930049.aspx

Marketing Budget Template – Free Template-easy-to-use
Excel marketing budget template to help you plan and
track your marketing expenses.
http://brandeo.drupalgardens.com/content/2014-marketing-
budget-template-free

Zig Ziglar- Attitude Makes All the Difference-
Motivational Video

John Maxwell – The Secret to Success – Motivational
Video

Best Motivational Speech Ever by Victor Antonio –
Motivational Video

Appendix:

5 Step Marketing Plan WORKSHEET

**To Get More Customers, Referrals
& Make More Money**

*A Winning Marketing Strategy for Small Businesses
By Violet James*

Date _____

Company _____

Name _____

Title _____

STEP 1- Know Your Competition & What Sets You Apart

Assignment #1

Who Are Your Competitors?

Conduct a **Competitive Comparison Analysis:**

List the (5) nearest direct competitors:
Company
Strengths *(What are they doing well?)*
Weaknesses *(What can I capitalize on?)*

_____

_____

_____

_____

_____

_____

_____

_____

_____

_____

_____

_____

_____

_____

_____

_____

What you need to know about your competitors:

Who are their clients?

_____

_____

_____

_____

_____

_____

_____

_____

_____

What fees are they charging, and how do your fees compare?

_____

_____

_____

_____

_____

_____

_____

_____

How are they advertising?

_____

_____

_____

_____

_____

_____

_____

_____

_____

**How do you differ from your competition? What makes you
Special/Unique? What can you offer that they don't?**

_____

_____

_____

_____

_____

_____

_____

_____

_____

_____

_____

_____

_____

_____

_____

_____

_____

_____

_____

_____

STEP 2- Know Your Customers

1- Who are your customers? *(age, gender, level of education, geographical location, annual income level, ethnicity, profession, industry, job title, etc.)*

_____

_____

_____

_____

_____

_____

_____

_____

_____

2- Pick a Niche? *If you target everybody then nobody is your ideal customer. Carve out a specific niche and dominate that niche. Examples—Lawyer that specializes in Divorce Law, Counselor that specializes in Child-Therapy, Dry Cleaners for the Metro-Detroit Area.*

_____

_____

_____

_____

_____

_____

3- List the patterns or habits your customers and potential customers share. *(where they shop, what they read, watch, listen to)*

_____

_____

_____

_____

_____

_____

_____

_____

4- Where can you find your ideal customer? *(associations, events, tradeshows, etc.)*

_____

_____

_____

_____

_____

_____

_____

_____

_____

_____

STEP 3 – Create a Compelling Marketing Message

See examples below on the difference between listing a service compared to offering benefits and results:

Listing Service & Things
versus
Offering Benefits & Results

Compare:
Designer Shoes
versus
 Comfort for your feet & the pleasure of walking

Books
versus
Hours of pleasure and the benefits of knowledge

Cottage
versus
Comfort and the quietness of a cozy place

Business Coaching
versus
Grow your company and improve performance

Assignment #3

Write a list of benefits and results that you offer your customers
(brainstorming)—

_____

_____

_____

_____

Dynamic Tag Lines

Examples:

McDonalds	…i'm lovin' it
Nike	…Just Do It
Allstate	…You're in good hands with Allstate
FedEx	…When you absolutely, positively need it there on time

Assignment #4

Create a Dynamic Tag Line *(brainstorming)—*

_____

_____

_____

_____

_____

Audio Logo (Elevator Speech)

An audio logo is a simple statement that answers the question, "What do you do?" Most people state their job title "I'm a designer" or "I'm a sales executive." The most effective way to answer that question is by using an audio logo.

"I help *(name your target audience)* to *(name one of the benefits or results you offer)."*

Examples—
I consult managers in developing leadership skills and performance
I teach children to stay healthy and fit

Create an Audio Logo *(brainstorming) If you have more than one target market you can create a different audio logo (elevator pitch) for each one.*

_____

_____

_____

_____

_____

_____

**Include your marketing message (tag line, benefits/results) in ALL your marketing materials and promotions.

STEP 4 - Determine a Marketing Budget and Marketing Mediums

Assignment #6

Develop your marketing budget *(If you have been in business for over a year, then you can easily track your marketing/advertising expense and budget. If you just started a business, then you will need to project an estimated figure).*
$_____ Annual budget

Assignment #7

Determine (1) to (3) marketing mediums that you will use *(A marketing medium is the vehicle/tool that you use to advertise and get your message out. Your goal is to choose a medium that targets your niche prospects at the lowest possible cost. You will want to keep track of results and drop marketing mediums that aren't doing well and add new ones until you discover the best marketing mediums that get you the desired goal for maximum referrals). Go to Step #4 in the book for a list of marketing mediums.*

_____
_____
_____
_____
_____
_____
_____

STEP 5 Focus on (2) Essential Customer Goals

In regards to customers there are (2) main goals:

> 1- Get new customers
> 2- Retain existing customers

#1 Get New Customers

Assignment #8

Develop (1) to (3) Action Plans to get new customers:

List (1) marketing strategy to get new customers *(use your assignment #7 answers as a reference) Go to Step #5 in the book for a list of examples of marketing strategies.*

ACTION PLAN #1*(brainstorming)* --

Strategy:_____

_____

_____

_____

_____

_____

_____

Goal *(desired outcome):*

_____

_____

Benefits of implementing this strategy:

_____

_____

_____

_____

_____

_____

Risks of implementing this strategy:

_____

_____

_____

_____

_____

_____

Potential obstacles and strategies for overcoming obstacles
(internal & external barriers):

_____

_____

_____

_____

_____

_____

_____

Potential Resources:

_____

_____

_____

_____

_____

_____

_____

Action Steps & Completion date(s):

_____

_____

_____

_____

_____

_____

_____

_____

_____

_____

_____

_____

_____

_____

ACTION PLAN #2 *(brainstorming)* --

Strategy:_____

_____

_____

_____

_____

_____

_____

Goal *(desired outcome)*:

_____

_____

_____

Benefits of implementing this strategy:

_____

_____

_____

_____

Risks of implementing this strategy:

_____

_____

_____

_____

Potential obstacles and strategies for overcoming obstacles

(internal & external barriers):

_____

_____

_____

_____

_____

_____

_____

_____

_____

_____

Potential Resources:

_____

_____

_____

_____

_____

_____

Action Steps & Completion date(s):

_____

_____

_____

ACTION PLAN #3 *(brainstorming)* --

Strategy:_____

_____

_____

_____

_____

Goal *(desired outcome)*:

_____

_____

_____

Benefits of implementing this strategy:

_____

_____

_____

_____

Risks of implementing this strategy:

_____

_____

_____

_____

_____

Potential obstacles and strategies for overcoming obstacles

(internal & external barriers):

_____

_____

_____

_____

_____

_____

_____

_____

Potential Resources:

_____

_____

_____

_____

_____

_____

Action Steps & Completion date(s):

_____

_____

_____

_____

_____

#2 Develop Action Plans on Retaining Existing Customers

Develop (1) to (3) Action Plans to Retain Existing Customers
Go to Step #5 in the book for a list of marketing strategies on how to have existing customers keep buying from you exclusively and more frequently.

ACTION PLAN #1 *(brainstorming)* --

Strategy:_____

_____

_____

_____

_____

_____

Goal *(desired outcome)*:

_____

_____

_____

_____

Benefits of implementing this strategy:

_____

_____

_____

_____

_____

Risks of implementing this strategy:

_____

_____

_____

_____

Potential obstacles and strategies for overcoming obstacles

(internal & external barriers):

_____

_____

_____

_____

_____

_____

_____

_____

_____

_____

Potential Resources:

_____

_____

_____

_____

_____

Action Steps & Completion date(s):

_____

_____

_____

_____

_____

_____

_____

_____

_____

_____

_____

_____

_____

ACTION PLAN #2 *(brainstorming)* --

Strategy:_____

_____

_____

_____

_____

_____

Goal *(desired outcome)*:

_____

_____

Benefits of implementing this strategy:

_____

_____

_____

_____

Risks of implementing this strategy:

_____

_____

_____

_____

Potential obstacles and strategies for overcoming obstacles

(internal & external barriers):

_____

_____

_____

_____

_____

_____

_____

_____

Potential Resources:

_____

_____

_____

_____

Action Steps & Completion date(s):

_____

_____

_____

_____

_____

_____

ACTION PLAN #3 *(brainstorming)* --

Strategy:_____

_____

_____

_____

_____

_____

Goal *(desired outcome)*:

_____

_____

Benefits of implementing this strategy:

_____

_____

_____

Risks of implementing this strategy:

_____

_____

_____

_____

_____

Potential obstacles and strategies for overcoming obstacles

(internal & external barriers):

_____

_____

_____

_____

_____

_____

_____

_____

Potential Resources:

_____

_____

_____

_____

Action Steps & Completion date(s):

_____

_____

_____

_____

_____

_____

About the Author

Violet James, MSM is an entrepreneur, marketing and business manager, award-winning web designer, and artist. She has over 20 years experience in business consulting, marketing and management. She is the cofounder and executive director of Christian-Kindle-Books.com NewDayCounseling.org and NewDayMusicOutreach.com. Violet is a best-selling author and has authored several books.

Connect with Violet James

It is my sincerest desire and hope *that (5) Step Marketing Plan To Get More Customers, Referrals & Make More Money - A Winning Marketing Strategy for Small Businesses* has helped you to create an effective, winning marketing plan that can take your business to the next level of success. I would love to hear your testimonials and how you have been helped. You can send your testimonials, feedback and comments to me at:

maxpotential312@gmail.com

I encourage you to share your experience, and I would truly appreciate if you would write a review on Amazon.com

My author profile:
http://www.amazon.com/author/violetjames

Join our *Words of Inspiration* page and Friend me on Facebook:
http://www.facebook.com/WordsOfInspiration

Follow and connect with us on Twitter:
http://www.twitter.com/behappy4lifeNDC

Visit the *Be Your Best* blog (offers RSS):
http://www.newdaycounselingcenter.blogspot.com/

LinkedIn: http://www.linkedin.com/in/violetjames

Other books by Violet James:

5 Simple Steps to Get Out of Debt: Live Debt-Free & Experience Financial Freedom

How to Start a Business: Step by Step Guide

www.ingramcontent.com/pod-product-compliance
Lightning Source LLC
Chambersburg PA
CBHW021442170526
45164CB00001B/359